SUCCESS WITH ORCHIDS

SUCCESS WITH ORCHIDS

WILMA RITTERSHAUSEN

WITH SPECIAL PHOTOGRAPHY BY
ERIC CRICHTON

TODTRI

In memory of Stan

This book was designed and produced by
TODTRI Book Publishers P.O. Box 572, New York,
NY 10116-0572 FAX: (212) 695-6984 e-mail: info@todtri.com

Visit us on the web! www.todtri.com

Printed and bound in Singapore

Library of Congress Catalog Card Number 97-066029
ISBN 1-57717-063-6

Author: Wilma Rittershausen

Publisher: Robert M. Tod
Designer: Vic Gilolitto
Art Director: Ron Pickless
Editor: Nicolas Wright
Project Editor: Ann Kirby
Typeset and DTP: Blanc Verso/UK

CONTENTS

FOREWORD

The orchid family is so vast that no single book can tell you everything, just as no one person can have knowledge of all there is to know about these incredible plants. Having spent a lifetime growing and writing about orchids, I can claim to know a little about these exquisite plants and am aware of the unique position that orchids hold at the top of the family tree of flowering plants.

The world of orchids is filled with beauty, but it also contains the most unusual, strange, and even bizarre flower forms. All are striking and worthy of further study, and for the more adventurous reader, there are many surprises waiting to be revealed.

This book is intended as a first voyage of discovery into a new and exciting floral world. I hope it will answer some of your questions, allay certain fears, ease some misconceptions, and convince you that it is possible to grow quite a number of delightful orchids easily and without special conditions in your greenhouse or home.

Right: *Cymbidium* **Angelica 'Advent.'** **Most orchids of the genus** *Cymbidium* **originated in tropical Asia, but enthusiasts now raise them on almost every continent.**

I have merely dipped into an ocean of precious gems to examine a few of the pearls. There are many more waiting to be found. I hope I have opened the door just a little to allow you to see inside; by opening the door even wider you could become captivated by the incredibility of the orchid family forever, as so many devotees have already experienced.

Wilma Rittershausen

Opposite: *Caularthron bicornutum* **from Collectamea Botanica by John Lindley, 1821.**

Right: *Dactylorhiza foliosa*. An attractive, hardy, terrestrial species which has naturalized in an attractive outdoor setting.

Phalaenopsis Joline 'Provence.' A standard type hybrid with lightly-dotted pink flowers of good shape. The flowers are long-lasting and the plant will grow in a warm room indoors or in a greenhouse.

PART ONE
THE ORCHID:
GROWING &
PROPAGATION

1
ORIGINS

Previous pages 10–11: *Phalaenopsis*
**Hennessy. A lovely, free-flowering,
peppermint-striped hybrid which will
bloom several times a year.**

Orchids are amazing! They are like no other plants on earth. With
at least 25,000 recognized species, they are just about the largest
family of flowering plants. They are also by far the most extraordinary and diverse. When you add a further 100,000 hybrids developed
over the last 150 years, you can see that we are looking at a remarkable
and highly successful group of plants.

Orchid species are wild, naturally occurring plants, which divide into
835 natural genera. To this figure can also be added approximately 1000
artificially man-made hybrid genera. No other plant has been so widely
hybridized or has proved to be so promiscuous in its breeding.

The orchid is highly developed in its flowers and vegetative parts and has
adapted to just about every environment; from equatorial forests, through
temperate climes, to the very edges of the polar regions. They are found
from sea level, across deserts and marshlands, to high mountain ridges.
The secret of this success lies in the orchid's ability to adapt, as well as its
unique pollination mechanism which, apart from a few exceptions, is totally reliant upon insects. Although orchids would have evolved along with
the insects millions of years ago, they are actually considered to be late
arrivals in evolutionary terms. This is borne out by the lack of fossil evi-
dence, and even today some orchids are still evolving.

This vast family, which has colonized every possible habitat worldwide,
has many varied and complex forms, which has resulted in a bewildering
variety of flower types produced by equally diverse plants. It is the orchid's
flowers which set it apart from all other plants. All are unique in their
structure but, no matter how diverse, all conform to one basic pattern.

THE ORCHID FLOWER

At the center of the orchid flower is the column. This is a single structure
which contains the male and female reproductive parts. At the end of the
column is the bright yellow pollen, packed into two, or sometimes more,
firm masses. These pollen masses, or pollinia, are hidden from view by a
protective cap, the anther-cap. On the underside of the column is situated
the female stigmatic surface in a small hollow. Surrounding the column are
three outer sepals, which more often resemble the petals, and three inner
petals. The third petal, at the bottom of the flower, has become modified
into a lip, or labellum. The purpose of this is to provide a landing area for

Right: *Cymbidium* **Stanley Fouracre x
Highlander. A standard type hybrid that
blooms in the early winter and produces
upright flower spikes.**

the alighting insect, who finds that there is a 'honey guide' indicating the way that it must go. In its search for nectar, which is not always given, the insect, most often a bee, effects pollination. As the bee pushes its way into the flower the anther-cap is dislodged and the pollen becomes attached to its head. The bee carries the pollen to the next flower where it is deposited onto the stigma. After fertilization the flower fades rapidly and the ovary behind the flower swells to become the seed capsule. This process can take up to nine months.

In the wild, the seed capsule ripens and splits along ridges causing slits to appear down its length. The seed trickles out and is carried by the wind, often for long distances. It is remarkably small, like fine sawdust, and a delicate pale gold. Just one seed capsule can contain up to a million seeds. If every seed germinated the world would long ago have been smothered with orchids. In reality, very few of these seeds germinate because the seed requires the association of a mycorrhiza, or microscopic fungus, to help it to grow.

The mycorrhiza also relies upon using the orchid seed as a host for its own development, so the two are interdependent and form a symbiotic relationship. The orchid seed, although ready to leave the capsule, is small,

Above: *Cattleya* Porcia. A free-flowering hybrid that blooms in the autumn and is suitable for the intermediate greenhouse.

Left: *Paphiopedilum* Clare de Lune. This beautiful Maudiae-type hybrid is one of the mottled-leaved types, which carry single flowers on a tall stem.

immature and lacking in chlorophyll or any food reserve such as is found in a pea or acorn. Both of these have, by comparison with the orchid seed, huge food resources to sustain the young growing shoot. It is the mycorrhiza therefore, which supplies the all-important nourishment to feed the orchid seed.

Of the thousands of seeds floating on the breeze, only very few, which happen to land where the mycorrhiza exists, can germinate and grow. Because orchids are perennial plants, they do not rely upon a vast annual renewal for the continuation of their species, so the very low success rate of seedlings is sufficient to ensure and maintain a healthy population in the wild.

Under cultivation, and using artificial methods known as asymbotic culture, every seed sown has an equal chance of germinating.

TERRESTRIAL, EPIPHYTIC, AND LITHOPHYTIC

Orchids are either terrestrial, epiphytic, or less often, lithophytic.

Terrestrial plants produce underground tubers (usually two), and a rosette of leaves in their season. The flowering stem rises from the center. Growth dies down after flowering and is renewed at the start of each growing season. Terrestrial orchids are found all over the world and flourish mainly in temperate to cold climates. They do not have the same appeal to growers as epiphytic orchids because their flowers are less flamboyant and their culture is not easy. Most enthusiasts are content to seek out and photograph the wild populations. A few are in cultivation where their specialized treatment can be met. Usually this entails growing them in a frost free alpine greenhouse, or, if conditions are not too severe, outside in a cold frame. Some of the most bizarre terrestrials are native to Australia, and these are certainly worth studying, through specialized books, if not actually in the field. In Britain there are approximately fifty species of terrestrial. Many of these are only just surviving as the increased use of chemicals in the countryside, along with more intensive agriculture, and the spread of urbanization depletes their habitats. Some botanical gardens are successfully raising these native plants from seed, and where possible, returning plants to the wild.

Epiphytic orchids are those which live on trees as air plants. They are not parasitic and take no nourishment from the host. They use the tree to gain height above the forest floor where there is less competition and more light. These plants are well adapted to life on a tree, and have developed special features to enable them to survive. Most produce pseudobulbs, or false bulbs, which are swollen stems containing water reserves to enable the plant to cope with long periods of drought. Thick, fleshy white aerial roots are produced in abundance. These secure the plant by adhering to the bark of the tree and hang freely to take up moisture which is stored in the pseudobulbs. These in turn support the leaves. Both pseudobulbs and leaves vary enormously in size and shape and also in the number of leaves to each pseudobulb.

Epiphytes can only thrive in warmer climates where exposed roots are not in danger of freezing. As the roots do not have the protection of soil around them, it is in the tropical areas close to the equator where the most exuberant and beautiful orchid species are found. These were the first to captivate the early Victorian growers in the Western world and they cultivated the cream of the New World's forests in huge, private collections. Today, many of those plants which seemed so abundant are no longer found in the wild, even where the original habitat remains, as the orchids have long since been collected out.

It is the epiphytic orchids which have generated by far the greatest interest for growers, and from which most of today's hybrids have been bred. They come in an astonishing variety of sizes, from tiny species which you could fit into a thimble (some *Pleurothallis*), to massive giants weighing over a ton which could bring down a huge ironwood tree by its sheer weight (*Grammatophyllum*). Most of those cultivated, however, are easily contained in a 6 to 12 inch pot (15 to 30 centimeters). The flowers of these epiphytic orchids are unbelievably diverse. While many are exquisitely beautiful, others are more aptly described as bizarre, even weird, or downright ugly and grotesque. Yet all are undeniably fascinating and can find devotees among orchid fanciers.

Lithophytic orchids are similar in appearance to the epiphytes, but dwell upon rocks rather than trees. Some epiphytes may grow either way. For cultivation purposes the lithophytes are treated the same as the epiphytes.

EARLY ORCHID COLLECTION

Two hundred years ago tropical orchids were unknown in the Western world. During the ages of discovery and expansion, when the British Navy commanded so much of the world's oceans, tales and actual specimens of hitherto

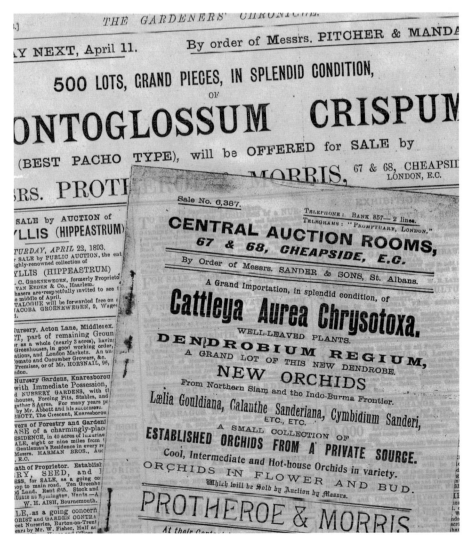

Above: An illustration of *Angraecum sesquipedale* from *The Gardeners' Chronicle* of 1893.

Left: Advertisement for orchid sales from *The Gardeners' Chronicle* of 1893 and a cover of an 1913 orchid sale catalogue.

Odontoglossum pescatorei 'Imperiale.'
From *Dictionaira Iconographique des Orchidees.*

unknown plant treasures began to arrive in Britain. The first reported tropical epiphytic orchid to arrive in Britain was named *Epidendrum* (meaning 'upon a tree'—as this was all the information known about it). When further orchids began to arrive, each with vastly differing characteristics, it became obvious that they could not all belong to the same genus, and so began the classifying of the different orchid genera.

But the early history of tropical orchids arriving in the Western world is, unfortunately, one of destruction, greed, and, for many orchids, death. Once it had become known that these beautiful plants existed in far-off lands, the Victorians wanted them in their own gardens and as a status symbol *par excellence*, to grace their large estates—many of which were maintained on the proceeds of the industrial revolution.

The early nurserymen were the first to send their collectors to South and central America in the New World, as well as to India and Nepal in the Old World, where they searched the mountain ranges of the Andes and Himalayas for the finest orchids. Later, the wealthy landowners of the huge estates sent their own collectors, and rivalry between collectors was intense. Whole areas would be cleared of orchids, the plants torn from the trees, and often felled for this one purpose. Collectors sought only the biggest plants to meet the demands of their employers. But small pieces and seedlings were not always spared, as these would be deliberately burnt on the spot to prevent rival collectors from having access to them.

The first orchids to survive the long sea voyages to England and Europe

Left: *Odontoglossum pescatorei*
'Leucoxanthum' from *Dictionaire*
Iconographique des Orchidees.

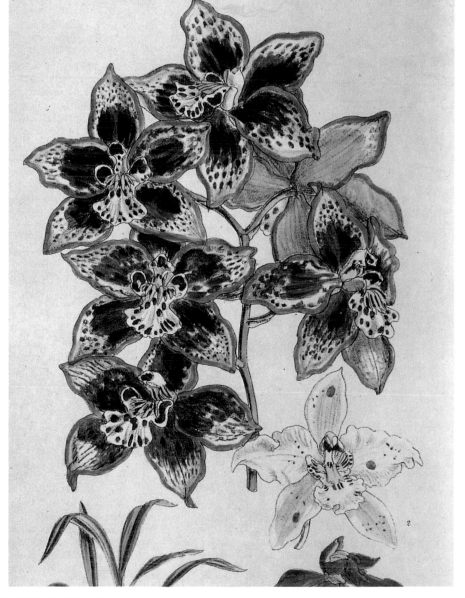

Left: *Odontioda* Vuylstekeae illustrated in
the *Botanical Magazine*, 1904, with its
parents, *Odontoglossum crispum* and
Cochlioda noezliana.

Left: *Lycaste* Aquila 'Detente.' A beautifully colored hybrid that produces blooms singly on the stem in early autumn.

often perished due to lack of knowledge about their requirements. Placed in dark, airless, and overheated 'ferneries', few survived to flower. But still the orchids came in the thousands, and soon specially built greenhouses were being designed, more suited to these cool growing, mountain dwelling plants. The Victorians went on to establish the largest private collections of orchids the world has ever seen, collections which have never since been equaled. They grew superb plants and established the art of orchid growing which has continued to this day.

Even after the decline of the large estates, orchid growing continued to gain in popularity but on a much smaller scale. The first hybrids appeared and rivaled the species for the attention of enthusiasts, while the importation of species became less (although new discoveries continued to cause excitement). Soon the hybrids, considered at first merely a novelty, outnumbered the species and gained in popularity.

PRESENT DAY

Orchid growing today has come within everyone's reach. More people than ever before are discovering the delights of cultivating some of the world's most beautiful flora. Modern methods of mass propagation (known as meristemming) has meant that the very finest varieties are available through specialist nurseries. The beginner has a wider choice available today than at any time before.

Meristemmed plants cost a fraction of the price that the original plants did years ago. In many cases, the modern complex hybrid has a pedigree going back over one hundred years. It is a tribute to the hybridizers' who have produced plants which are heat tolerant, enabling them to be grown in hotter parts of the world. They have a built-in hybrid vigor and free flowering habit, often blooming two or three times in one year.

Today the would-be orchid grower does not have to look far for advice. Amateur orchid societies abound, and other growers are always delighted to share their knowledge, and sometimes propagations, with new enthusiasts. Orchid shows and conferences are regular features of the horticultural calendar, where plants can be purchased and the experts consulted. There are orchids for the indoor windowsill, sun lounge, or greenhouse, and they can be purchased in bud to produce blooms soon after, thereby inspiring the newcomer to acquire ever more varieties.

Facing Page: *Paphiopedilum* Cyclops 'Superba.' An older type of hybrid with a striking flower with a heavily spotted dorsal, it is still very popular today.

2
WHERE TO GROW

Growing orchids is really quite simple. You do not need elaborate accommodation or equipment. Many orchids will be quite happy on a windowsill indoors or, for a wider choice of plants, an ordinary greenhouse will be quite suitable.

In various parts of the world, the same plants can be grown by applying different methods of controlling their environment. In tropical climates, for instance, it will only be necessary to erect a shade house as protection from the sun, and all heat is free! In countries where snow can cover the ground for months on end, cellar culture is practiced with success. Here the plants are grown in insulated quarters under artificial lights which provide most of the warmth needed for the subterranean growing area.

Wherever orchids are grown their basic needs remain the same. Many growers begin with a few plants in the home and later, when the collection has inevitably grown to numbers which threaten to take over the house, erect a greenhouse solely for their needs. Otherwise, orchids can be grown alongside any other plants which are compatible (but please note that they would not do well growing with a tomato crop!).

INDOORS OR OUTDOORS?

In many parts of the world, including Britain, summer temperatures are warm enough to enable some orchids to be grown outside for a few weeks of the year. This can benefit those plants which will gain from the extra light and cooler temperatures available outdoors rather than being in a small greenhouse, which can easily overheat in daytime.

Within the home there are many places where orchids will thrive. Ideally, you need a south facing window to gain the most light. If the plants are kept close to the glass they will need to be shaded from the summer sun. Net curtains should provide sufficient protection, or the plants can be moved further into the room. An east or west facing window can be just as good, giving sufficient light but less direct sun—possibly better in summer, but less beneficial in winter. A north facing window may be a good alternative in summer, but it would not provide much light in winter. Each window can also have further advantages depending upon the location and outside area. For example, a south facing window with a tree directly outside may afford sufficient shade. Plants can also be moved to different quarters

Right: Orchids growing indoors on a window sill need to be provided with humidity trays to maintain some moisture around them. These are standing on upturned pots.

according to the season. Some orchids require less light and these can be grown inside the room where a suitable place is available.

Locations for plants which should be avoided are draughty areas or areas close to sources of heat, such as a radiator, stove, and even the television set. An older type of house may not have an obviously suitable area, or you may prefer to grow your orchids where they can be most admired, which might even be a dark corner. For this an indoor growing case may be the answer, which can be fitted out with horticultural strip-lighting and glass-fronted doors. This can easily become a permanent home for a number of smaller growing orchids.

The bathroom is often considered a good growing area, but it is usually

Below: A trellis makes an attractive display place for blooming orchids.

the least well-lit room in the house, with the light level being unsuitable. In addition, rapid changes in temperature and humidity also occur here. Besides, how would you like to live in your bathroom? I have seen bathroom grown orchids whose leaves have become white with regular applications of talcum powder!

The kitchen is a far better option, provided that the cooking activities do not cause sudden increases in temperature. The spare room may have more space and the family cats can be kept away from the plants, but spare rooms are usually unheated and in winter can be barren places, cold by day and night. Even in summer, the temperature may not rise sufficiently during the day for optimum growth. Your orchids will thrive best in a comfortable room where the temperature varies slightly during both day and night, never getting too hot nor too cold.

LOOKING AFTER YOUR PLANTS

Having selected the area where your orchids are to grow, you need to provide them with their own micro-climate. This is achieved by placing the plants on a humidity tray covered with pebbles which are kept wet. The water level can be just below the pebbles so that the orchids are not standing in water, but have moisture rising around them from evaporation. If you have only one or two orchids, surround them with other green plants such as ferns to create a better growing environment. One small plant on its own is less likely to succeed. Plants always grow better in groups.

To prevent water spillage over the tray, it may be necessary to remove the

Above: Many orchids can be successfully cultivated in an indoor growing case, which automatically controls the light and temperature.

25

Previous pages 26–27: In a greenhouse, some orchids can be grown on a tiered staging, while others can be placed on shelves above or hung from the sides to conserve space.

plants to the kitchen sink for watering and then return them to their growing area when they have drained. An alternative is to use a deeper, house-plant trough in which the plants can be stood on upturned saucers or half pots to keep the rim of the pot level with the rim of the trough, and well above the water level. Having created a suitable growing area, regular spraying, watering, and feeding must be routine in order to maintain successful culture in the home.

THE GREENHOUSE

The ideal greenhouse will be sited running west to east to take full advantage of available light. If you are building a greenhouse specially for orchids, you do not need the glass to extend right down to the ground. The orchids will be grown on staging so light below this is not a necessity. A brick base will also keep the greenhouse warmer. Where a greenhouse is already in situ and has glass sides, these can be closed in with polystyrene panels or similar materials to aid insulation. An earth floor is better than a cemented one, it will be easier to keep wet and provides a better atmosphere for the orchids. Low light, ground hugging plants including ferns and brightly colored impatiens can be planted out in this floor area. As well as looking attractive, this helps to maintain humidity.

An open, slatted staging is ideal for the orchids, and tiered where room permits. This allows free air movement around the plants. Alternatives are sheet staging covered with gravel which is kept wet. Greenhouses come with sufficient ventilation in the roof, and for orchids, it is an advantage to have bottom vents as well. Used together they provide a good flow of cooling air in summer. On hot days the door can be left open to prevent overheating.

The greenhouse will need a heating system capable of maintaining the required temperatures without being at full stretch. Various forms of heating are available, with the best being run by electricity. An electric fan heater will keep the air moving and can be used to blow cold air in the summer.

Do not allow the warm air to blow directly onto the plants. Place the heater at floor level at one end where the moving air can circulate. A tray of water placed in front of the heater will add moisture to the air. Remember that gas and paraffin heaters can emit harmful fumes and are not really suitable for orchids.

If you have a conservatory, sun lounge, or lean-to greenhouse attached to the house, the central heating system can be extended into that area, with the installation of an additional radiator at very little extra cost.

In greenhouses, sun lounges, and conservatories the glass will need to be shaded during the summer months. Paint shading is the first step, but may not be sufficient on its own. Netting may be used as well and this can be put on the inside or the outside of the glass, while the paint should be put on the outside. The netting needs to be a few inches or centimeters from the glass to allow for a flow of cooling air between netting and glass. As a rough guide, if you can look at the sun through the shading, it should be sufficient. By the end of the summer the paint shading on the outside will have been much reduced by rain and weather conditions. Clean off any remaining paint and take down the netting in order to give the orchids full light throughout the winter months. The shading will not be needed again until the sun becomes stronger.

Right: *Cymbidium* **Elismon produces many flowers on an arching spike, and is ideal for gowing indoors.**

Paphiopedilum insigne. **This species, once very common, is now considerably rare in collections. It has produced many hundreds of hybrids, and originates from India.**

Small greenhouses can be difficult to control in summer. Rapid temperature fluctuations and overheating can make them a dangerous place for orchids. If you are not on hand during the day to ensure that the greenhouse remains cool enough, one option is to remove the orchids to an outdoor location for the summer. The result will be a much hardier plant growth, which will encourage better flowering. A suitable place needs to be found, ideally on a bench alongside a fence or wall where the plants will get the morning or late afternoon sun, but they must be shaded from the midday sun. Underneath a tree, for instance, may provide the ideal spot, but bear in mind that here aphids and other unwanted insects can drop onto the orchids from above.

Orchids can be placed outdoors once all danger of frost has passed, and returned to the greenhouse or home well before the first frost of winter is expected. While the greenhouse is empty it can be cleaned out and any repairs undertaken.

Plants situated outdoors will dry out much quicker from being exposed to the sun and wind and will need more watering. The extra light will increase the growth, so extra feed can be given. On suitable days, when there is no rain, the orchids can be liberally sprayed from overhead with water. This can be done several times a day when drying out is rapid, but always make sure that the foliage is dry by the time the sun no longer shines on the plants and the temperature starts to drop.

During periods of low temperatures and constant rain, it may become necessary to cover the plants temporarily to avoid saturating the compost. However, as wind very often follows rain, this should rarely cause a major problem. Small pots which may otherwise be blown over by strong winds need to be placed inside a heavier container, or suspended from an overhead railing.

GROWING TEMPERATURES

Orchids are divided into three groups depending upon where they originate in the wild, and especially the altitude at which they grow. These can be classed as cool, intermediate and warm, or hot house.

Cool growing varieties need a minimum winter night temperature of 50°F (10°C) and a summer day maximum of 75–80°F (24–27°C). The intermediate section require a 5°F (3°C) higher minimum, and the warm-growing types need a minimum in winter of 60–65°F (16–19°) rising to 85–90°F (29–32°C) on a summer day. No orchids like to be too cold or too warm, and excessive temperatures over a prolonged period can cause stress and the plants will suffer. Ideally there should be a minimum difference of 10°F (6°C) between night and day. For most of the year the variation will be greater, which is fine.

Humidity is important to orchids, but this must balance the temperature. When the temperature is low, let the greenhouse dry out. When the temperature is high, damp down more often. Damping down means soaking the greenhouse floor and staging to create a good growing atmosphere. Damping down is done all year round, less in winter, and always when the temperature is rising.

Overhead spraying can be done daily in summer, and occasionally in winter when it is sunny and the water will not linger on the foliage too long. Indoor plants can be sprayed more lightly using a fine-nozzle hand-held spray. You should do this several times a day in summer but much less in winter. Alternatively, wipe the foliage with a wet tissue to keep it dust-free.

Watering is best done using a spouted water-can or, in a larger collection, a lance on the end of a hose. Pour water liberally over the surface of the pot, once or twice, to ensure enough has been absorbed by the compost. Keep the plants evenly moist while growing in order to avoid getting them too wet or too dry at any particular time. Those orchids which rest in the winter can be dried out between waterings. Until the new growth starts in the spring, the orchids inside the home will need more watering than those in the greenhouse.

Liquid feed is usually given at every third watering, using an orchid feed prepared to the instructions on the packet.

3
ℋOW TO GROW

Orchids are perennial plants. With care and regular attention they can live for many years and, like a shrub or tree purchased for the garden, can be considered a permanent and continuously growing acquisition. Once maturity has been reached (when the plant is about five years of age), old growth or pseudobulbs will die and be replaced by new ones.

PSEUDOBULBS

The pseudobulbs are the most robust part of the plant, living longer than the leaves or roots which are partially replaced at the start of each growing season. A typical evergreen orchid such as a *Cymbidium* will consist of several pseudobulbs which are attached to each other by an underground rhizome, the younger pseudobulbs being in leaf and the older ones leafless. The leaves from one pseudobulb are usually shed after two to four years. They may drop all at once or, more often, one or two at a time over a few years. Most leaf-loss occurs at the end of the growing season as the plant prepares for its resting period.

Not all orchids produce pseudobulbs. The best known, among those with a different growth habit, are the phalaenopsis and vandas. Here, pairs of leaves extend from a central growing tip on a continuously upward-growing rhizome. In phalaenopsis the rhizome is short with the broad, oval leaves being produced one at a time, so that an average plant will consist of four to five leaves at any time. Vandas grow much taller. Their stiffened, narrow leaves form pairs along the stem. Both phalaenopsis and vandas are evergreen.

Deciduous orchids such as lycastes lose their season's foliage quite rapidly and remain in a leafless, dormant state during the winter.

GROWING HABITS

All orchids have a growing season followed by a resting period. The new growths start in the early spring, activated by the lengthening daylight and slightly higher temperatures. A small green shoot will be seen at the base of the leading (youngest) pseudobulb or growth which will gradually extend, fanning out into individual leaves until the full length is attained. The base begins to fill out and swells during the growing season to its

Right: *Paphiopedilum purpuratum*. A species of the mottled-leaved type, which produces its flowers during the autumn. It originates from Hong Kong.

32

eventual size. This is the new pseudobulb. New roots will follow shortly after the new growth is seen. Thus each season's growth is self-sustaining, although dependent upon the whole of the plant for its strength and vigor. To divide a plant into single pseudobulbs would be to destroy this collective strength. While most of the pseudobulbs would produce new growth from spare dormant eyes, with limited reserves to sustain growth, it would be several years before each piece could be expected to bloom. For this reason plants are kept to at least four pseudobulbs (and often many more), provided there are always more pseudobulbs still in leaf rather than leafless. When an excess of leafless pseudobulbs have accumulated on a plant, the oldest ones are removed at repotting time, so that the balance of the plant is maintained. Too many leafless pseudobulbs can become a burden on the plant. These severed pseudobulbs can be divided singly and when potted up will provide propagations, growing from the spare eyes at the base.

Deciduous types such as lycastes and anguloas are exceptions where a cluster of leafless pseudobulbs with only the current season's in leaf is normal. Some types, however, including the deciduous calanthes and pleiones produce pseudobulbs which are not long lived and which die naturally within one or two seasons. Here, a large plant cannot be achieved in the same way, although a number of unattached pseudobulbs can be grown together in one pot to produce the effect of a specimen plant.

Large specimen plants are the result of years of good culture and can be achieved with all orchids by not splitting them into smaller divisions. Many orchids cannot be seen at their full potential until they reach specimen size. In any collection a few specimen plants can prove their worth with their superior flowering display, and are a testament to the grower's skill.

Orchids bloom at different times of the year in their season. The flower spikes almost always come from the newest pseudobulbs. Generally the older, flowered pseudobulbs will not produce spikes again. Depending upon the type of orchid, the flower spike may be produced from the base of the made-up pseudobulbs at the end of the growing season (as with cymbidiums), or at the start of the growing season, when the new growth is young (as seen in some odontoglossums). With miltoniopsis the flower spike can be looked for at any time after the new growth is halfway to maturity. Cattleyas produce their spikes after the pseudobulb has matured from within the protective sheaths at the top of the tall, club-shaped pseudobulbs. Encyclias also flower from the apex of the pseudobulbs, as do many others. Flower spikes on *Phalaenopsis* appear at the base of the last completed leaf, as with vandas and other similar upward-growing types. The paphiopedilums produce their buds from stems which emerge from the center of the newly completed growth.

Orchids are at rest when the plant ceases to grow and it becomes dormant. During this time they will require very little water. Some orchids may rest for several weeks or even months, while others make do with a very short period, which often passes unnoticed by the grower. A plant is at rest when there are no signs of active growth. Roots which have extended green tips when active become closed over with the white covering, or velamen, which follows behind the growing tip.

Hybrids among the cymbidiums and *Odontoglossum* alliance have very short resting periods, so that watering need hardly be reduced in winter. Coelogynes, encyclias and dendrobiums all have long resting periods when they can safely be allowed to dry out for short periods.

WHICH ORCHIDS TO GROW?

With so many orchid types to choose from it can be bewildering for the beginner to know which plants to choose to start a collection. Obviously, some orchids are easier to grow then others, and much depends upon personal choice. Appreciation varies, and orchids can be found to suit all tastes. The most popular orchids which can be considered among the beginners' range are the cymbidiums, particularly the miniature varieties. These are more compact in size, and are also more free-flowering. They are equally at home either indoors or in a cool greenhouse. They come in a wide range of colors and the flowers will last up to eight weeks, often blooming throughout the winter.

For exquisite flower patternings and markings, the odontoglossums are unequaled. Interbreeding of related genera has provided an endless variety of colors, shapes, and sizes on plants of a uniform stature, all loosely termed odontoglossums. They like cool, airy conditions and will grow almost anywhere. Their flowering is at various times of the year, some blooming every nine months or so, as their season's growth is completed.

Dendrobiums are a colorful genus, and extremely varied. The cool-grow-

Osmoglossum pulchellum. **Many of the smaller growing species are at their best when grown to specimen size, as is this very fragrant plant.**

ing *Dendrobium nobile* type hybrids are very distinct and give beautifully fanciful flowers in a wide range of colors. Their culture is more challenging as they need high summer temperatures and much cooler, dryer winters to initiate the flower buds. They bloom in the spring following a long rest and the flowers come on short stems grouped along the length of their canes, or extended pseudobulbs.

If your choice is for miniature orchids, look for some of the smaller growing coelogynes and encyclias. Here can be found little beauties such as *Coelogyne ochracea*, with pristine white, scented flowers. Delightful encyclias include the creamy colored, highly fragrant *Encyclia lancifolia* and *E. radiata*. Maxillarias can be especially colorful, and particularly hard to beat is the pretty *Maxillaria picta*, with its yellow flowers flecked with red and carrying a sweet fragrance. These are all cool growing orchids ideally suited to windowsill culture.

By far the most popular orchids for a warm room indoors or a warmly heated greenhouse are the phalaenopsis. These easily manageable plants provide blooms up to three times a year, on long lasting flower spikes in shades of pink, white, and yellow. Following closely behind for popularity and ease of culture are the miltoniopsis, the colorful 'Pansy Orchids' with their large, flat-faced flowers on modest-sized plants. Two main flowering seasons in early and late summer provide an abundance of blooms in red, pink, white and yellow, with numerous delicate markings on the lips. Their fragrance is an added bonus. Equally at home beside them are the paphiopedilums, known as 'Slipper Orchids' because of their distinctive pouch. Their dramatic flowers are mostly single on the stem arising from the center of a rosette of leaves. Bold colors and striped markings are often intermingled, with green, red, bronze, and brooding dark shades most often seen. Multi-flowered types carry much taller stems from which to exploit their blooms. They are mainly winter flowering and very long lasting. The attractive leaves may be plain or mottled green.

Enjoying similar warm temperatures but preferring a lighter aspect, are the cattleyas and related orchids. Cattleyas refer loosely to a whole group of interbred orchids which have produced a wonderful range of available plants. Although the plants can be large and unwieldy, the flamboyant blooms are the largest among the cultivated orchids. Colors range from white, pink, and yellow, to cerise and lavender-purple, and the flowers are produced in spring and late summer.

Left: *Oncidium* Tiger Wyld 'Babe.' Hundreds of flowers are produced by this hybrid, which needs plenty of headroom while in bloom.

4
POTTING &
PROPAGATION

Right: Orchids can be grown in a variety of baskets in addition to the usual pots. Plants in baskets can easily be suspended from the greenhouse roof.

While the vast majority of cultivated orchids are epiphytes, or have been bred from epiphytic species, and are more used to an open air life attached to a tree, we grow our orchids in pots. This is by far the most convenient method of containing them, although it is possible to grow some species suspended in open baskets, and on hanging slabs of bark, where they quickly adapt to a more natural way of life. Plants grown in this way are more suited to greenhouse culture where a high humidity will encourage the aerial roots, but extra water will be needed to keep the plants moist. Therefore regular overall spraying and dipping is essential. Plants with untidy or straggly growth habits can be accommodated more easily on bark, where they look very attractive. There is also the added pleasure of watching active roots grow, and they can safely remain undisturbed for years.

COMPOSTS

When grown in pots, orchids require an open, well-drained compost and there are many opinions on what this should be. The most straightforward growing material is pine bark chippings. This is obtained from the cropping of mature trees and is sold in different grades by specialist orchid nurseries and some garden centers. Additional materials can be added such as horticultural charcoal to keep the compost sweet; Cornish grit or other aggregate to prevent clogging; also *Sphagnum* moss or peat to retain extra moisture. This basic organic compost will provide the plant with most of the nutrients required for healthy growth, and a little additional supplementary feeding is all that is necessary.

An alternative popular growing material is the man-made fiber Rockwool. Orchids potted in this inorganic compound can grow very well, but are totally dependent upon an artificial feed supplied to the pot on a regular basis. Being inorganic, there is no decomposition that takes place, and it is therefore possible to keep the compost much wetter without the danger of rotting roots. The plants are loosely potted and only need moving when they have outgrown their pots.

REPOTTING AND DROPPING-ON

Flowering sized orchids require repotting every two years. By this time they will have used up the natural food in the compost, and will have out-

Top left: This plant has grown over the edge of the pot and needs repotting. This is the right time as new growth is showing. *Top right*: Plastic pots can be squeezed to release the plant, or use a knife around the inside of the rim. *Second row, left*: The plant has been taken out of the pot it had outgrown—note the tight ball roots. The old bracts around the base are trimmed off. *Second row, right*: The new pot is two sizes larger to allow for growth. Polystyrene chips are used in the base for drainage. *Third row, left*: The plant is placed in the new pot with the oldest pseudobulbs to one side. *Third row, right*: Compost is added, being careful not to bury the plant too deep; the pseudobulbs and new growth should 'sit' on the compost. *Bottom left:* The remainder of the compost is added with minimum disturbance to the plant. *Bottom center:* The compost is pushed down gently with the fingers. *Bottom right:* The compost should be just below the rim to allow for future watering. Remember to replace the label.

grown their pots. This can be seen when the leading pseudobulbs have reached the edge of the pot, or are actually over the rim. The plant may also have pushed itself up by the roots so that is stands high in the pot. Alternatively, the compost will have become too broken-down to be of any further use and can be detrimental to the roots by not allowing sufficient air around them. If you can push your finger into the compost, it needs replacing.

The best time to repot is in the spring. Plants flowering at this time can be repotted immediately after flowering. Ideally, the new growth should just be showing, but the new roots will not have started. Therefore, when the roots do appear they will have the advantage of growing into fresh compost without any further disturbance. Young plants, including seedlings and propagations will need 'dropping-on' every six months for the first year or two. Dropping-on means placing a plant into a larger pot without disturbing or trimming the root-ball. This will ensure a steady rate of growth until they reach flowering size. Late summer is the alternative time to attend to these and any other young mature plants which can ben-efit from this. It is possible with all young plants and certain older ones where the compost is in a good condition and capable of lasting another year or so.

Plants growing in Rockwool can be potted at almost any time of the year provided there is no disturbance to the roots, although it is better to avoid doing this during either the hottest or coldest months.

A young mature plant is one with about four or five pseudobulbs, all or most in leaf. Such a plant will not need any reduction of its pseudobulbs, neither will it be large enough to divide. Provided the compost is in good condition it can be simply dropped-on into a pot 2 inches (9 centimeters) larger. Have ready fresh compost (which has been previously dampened), the new pot, and a quantity of polystyrene pieces to use for crocking in the base of the pot. Remove the plant label and the plant from the pot. A few sharp taps on the edge of the bench to the pot rim should release the plant and allow it to be slid out of the pot. Otherwise, take a long-bladed knife and slide it around the pot rim until the plant is free. This is also a very good time to examine the roots which should be firm and white, with the growing tips white to pale green, almost translucent. There can be so many roots that no compost is visible and the root-ball has become solid. If any roots are found to be blackened, soft and sodden, (where the outer cover-ing peels easily away to leave the thin wiry center thread) they are dead, and they need to be cut right back to the base of the plant.

Providing the rootball is in good condition, it is a simple procedure to position the plant in the new pot on top of a layer of the crocking material. Hold the plant so that the oldest pseudobulbs are against the side of the pot leaving maximum room between the new growth and the other side of the pot. This gap is so that the plant can grow forward over the next year or two. The base of the leading growth should be just below the pot rim. Some orchid species have a tendency to produce each pseudobulb slightly above the previous one, as it climbs ever higher. Here it may be necessary to bury the older pseudobulbs in order that the leading one is not left high and dry. Pour in handfuls of compost, and if bark, press down firmly by pushing it well down around the pot rim with the fingers. If you are using Rockwool fiber, pour this in loosely and settle it down by tapping the pot on the bench. This material does not need to be pressed down too hard.

Following pages 42–43: *Odontoglossum* **Heonum. A beautifully colored hybrid suitable for a cool greenhouse. This plant will bloom over a long period at almost any time of the year.**

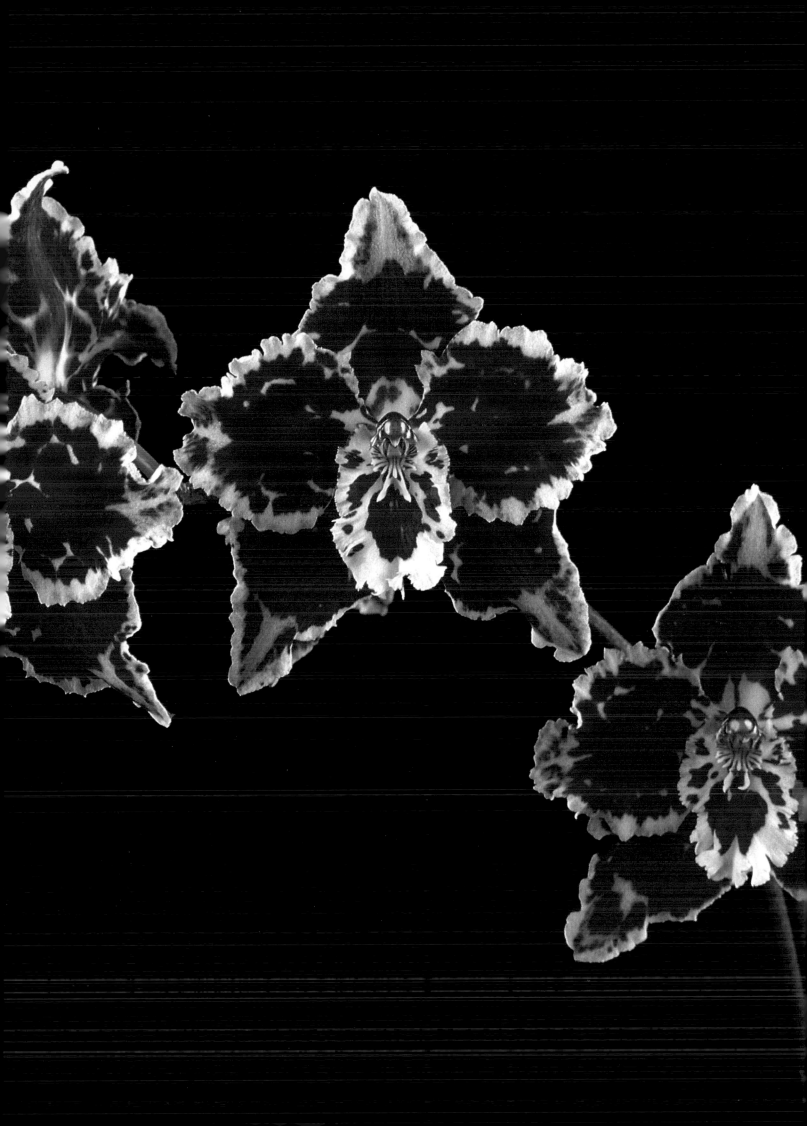

When you have finished the plant should be standing firm in the pot. Tall plants such as dendrobiums may need staking to ensure they are held firm until new roots have anchored them.

Plants with more than four pseudobulbs can be reduced to this size if required, by removing the excess leafless pseudobulbs from the back. Once the plant is out of its pot, you can sever the backbulbs by cutting through the rhizome which joins them. Cut right through the root ball and remove all the dead roots, cutting back to the base of the plant. Split the oldest pseudobulbs up singly and pot-up individually, or even collectively, to use for propagating. Take the front, growing part of the plant and trim the live roots back to about 6 inches (15 centimeters) long. This division can now be potted as previously described, tucking the roots in underneath and filling in with compost all round, making sure the plant ends up firm in its pot.

Where a plant has grown to a size with more than eight pseudobulbs and has new growths on more than one front, it can easily be split into two equal parts, each with at least four pseudobulbs and one leading growth. This will not reduce the plant to less than that needed for it to bloom again in the next season. The above procedure can be followed, dividing the plant at the center to produce the desired size.

Examples of species which grow in an upward direction, producing one pseudobulb above the previous one, are *Oncidium flexuosum* and *Maxillaria tenuifolia*. Instead of burying half the plant in a pot, try growing it on a slab of tree-fern or cork bark, with a wire hook at the top for hanging. Remove all old compost so that the plant is bare-rooted. Remove all dead roots and trim the live ones. (Unless they were made outside of the pot, in which case, leave well alone.) Using thin plastic-coated wire, secure the plant to the slab by placing the oldest pseudobulbs at the bottom and leaving sufficient space for the plant to continue its upward habit on the slab. If using tree-fern the plant will root easily into this. With cork bark you will need a moisture pad of *Sphagnum* moss or an alternative material placed beneath the plant for it to root into. The roots will also trail over the cork bark and extend freely into the air. Once these new roots are seen, spray them daily to encourage a good mass of growth.

Yet another alternative is to grow a plant in a wooden or plastic water-lily basket. This is essential for stanhopeas whose flower spikes grow downward through the compost to emerge at the bottom of the basket.

These various methods of containing orchids add interest to any collection, and also add enjoyment to the growing of them.

A few days after repotting, water sparingly and then resume normal watering and feeding. Some of the plants may drop a few leaves after repotting.

Left: *Paphiopedilum parishii*. One of the most striking of the multi-flowered species which blooms mainly through the winter months. The plant originates from Burma and Thailand.

5
PESTS &
DISEASES

Some pests can be annoying, others harmful, but all should be prevented from becoming a major concern on the orchids. Springtime is usually associated with an increase in unwanted pests which for many of them is often the start of their breeding season. The higher temperatures triggering an increase in their activity. Most orchid pests can be controlled without resorting to the use of toxic chemicals.

In the greenhouse some pests will become resident, and numbers will, from time to time, increase rapidly if conditions are favorable. Other pests enter the orchids' growing area through open windows when conditions outside permit their breeding.

Aphids will appear on buds, flower spikes, and the leaves of young growths. They are sap-sucking pests which can cause severe damage if their numbers are allowed to go unchecked. They leave puncture wounds on the buds which will grow with the buds causing large bumpy areas on the sepals of the flowers. On new growths their damage causes yellowish areas which later become blackened as infection sets into the damaged tissue. Aphids are comparatively large insects, and they should be continually watched out for and destroyed before they can build up large colonies, when they could become a serious pest. Aphids can be removed by dipping the effected areas in lukewarm water to which has been added a little detergent, then swilled around until all aphids have been dislodged. Alternatively, syringe the greenfly with a hand-held spray bottle of the solution. Where young growths are infected and you do not want to get water inside the leaves, sweep up the greenfly with a small artist's paint brush. Repeat on a daily basis until all the adults and newly hatched young have been eradicated. Aphids will also leave a sticky residue on the leaves which will encourage fungus to grow on the sugary surface. Ants are also encouraged to 'milk' them, and will carry individuals from one plant to another to maintain the 'herd.'

Slugs and snails will also thrive in the warm, moist atmosphere of an orchid house. Frogs and toads, however, are natural pest controllers which will often take up residence under the staging, emerging to forage on regular nightly patrols. Provided slug pellets are not used, both toads and frogs will offer a valuable service. In addition you can supplement their activity by putting out slices of apple or potato. Small bush snails will congregate underneath those areas overnight. Searching after dark with a

Right: *Vanda* **Thonglor. One of the many fantastic hybrids suitable for a warm greenhouse. The plant likes to be grown in good light and is mainly summer flowering.**

Odontioda Red Devon. The rich red coloring of this hybrid is the result of crossing *Odontoglossum* with *Cochlioda.*

torch in hand remains one of the best ways of catching these pests. The damage done to flower spikes, new growths, root tips, and pseudobulbs can be extensive. Use cotton wool wraps around the base of growing flower spikes. Slugs and snails will not be able to cross this. Maturing pseudobulbs can be attacked by garden snails which can cause a large hole to appear overnight, and the raw area will ooze a type of sticky glue. If this occurs, lay the plant on its side and clean out the wound with a kitchen tissue. Using horticultural sulfur, pack the wound by pressing the sulfur well into it and avoid getting it wet until healed. All slug holes can be treated this way to dry up the affected area and prevent infection. But, unfortunately, when the damage is done, it cannot be disguised.

Mice, bumble bees, and even Blue Tits can all be responsible for taking pollen from flowers. Mice and small birds find it particularly nutritious and will even break into a bud to steal the pollen. Bees, of course, dislodge the pollen while seeking nectar within the flower. Once the pollen has been removed the orchid flower blushes red and wilts, and a flower which should have been enjoyed for weeks on end is finished in a few days. Humane mouse traps are available allowing the little creature to be released well away from the greenhouse. Bees and Blue Tits can be prevented from entering the greenhouse by attaching a mesh gauze to the inside area of the ventilators.

Ants, woodlice, and whitefly larvae can destroy compost by breaking it down until it becomes clogged with dust-fine particles. This, in turn, makes it impossible for the water to drain through or for the roots to breathe, and they will die. Woodlice and whitefly larvae will also attack the roots of very young seedlings. Both these pests live in damp areas under the staging. Using a weak solution of Jayes Fluid in a rosed water-can, soak the floor and water the affected plants. Repeating this after a few days should destroy further generations.

Perhaps the worst pests of all are those which are so small they are hard to see. Usually, it is the damage caused by their large numbers which first alerts the grower to their presence. The Red Spider Mite is hardly discernible with the naked eye, but under a magnifying glass it is a reddish-orange mite which can travel surprisingly fast across a leaf surface. Large colonies attack the undersides of leaves on cymbidiums and almost any other soft-leafed orchid. Look for a silvery-white clouding on the underside of the foliage, and fine webbing between the buds on flower spikes. Bad infestations of Red Spider Mite can destroy a plant, causing premature leaf loss where the foliage is so badly damaged it cannot recover. Leaves with silvery undersides will later turn black as infection sets in the damaged leaf cells. Once this pest has built up a large population it can be extremely difficult to eradicate, and fumigation will have to be resorted to. Always read the manufacturer's instructions on the cone carefully and take all necessary precautions. Where the pest is detected in the early stages, it can be got rid of by cleaning the affected plant with methylated spirits. Using a paper tissue dipped in the alcohol, wipe each leaf in turn, then wash off with clean water. Repeat as often as necessary.

There are various scale insects which will attack orchids, often hiding away beneath sheath-bracts where they can build up into large colonies before detection. In particular, they are often found on the pseudobulbs of cattleyas, underneath the sheathing. They are sometimes white, covered in a woolly membrane, or brown. There are hard scale and soft scale, and all are recognizable by the small round or oval shell under which the adults live and produce their young. Damage to the plants can be seen in round yellow blotches on the leaves. Remove this pest by using an old toothbrush dipped in methylated spirits to dislodge the scale, and then wash off with clean water. Scrub gently to avoid scratching the leaf surface.

Mealy bug is a soft-bodied pink insect which covers itself in a woolly substance, which at first glance looks not unlike woolly scale. A dab of methylated spirits on this pest immediately shows it to be different. Again, ugly yellow blotches will reveal its presence when it is usually found on the undersides of leaves, in the axils, and other hard-to-reach places. It will also get onto the flower buds. Red Spider Mite, scale insects, and mealy bug are all sapsucking creatures which can puncture the leaf surface leaving it venerable to infection and virus disease.

Fungal infections attack damaged tissue and will cause these areas to turn black. Virus diseases will attack healthy tissue, leaving white streaks, often with a diamond pattern on the young leaves. As the leaves age, the lines become more noticeable as they turn black from the fungal infection. There is no cure for virus, which can be spread by the sapsucking pests. Affected plants are best kept well away from the other orchids,

or destroyed. Such plants should definitely not be given away to an unsuspecting friend.

Other problems to beset orchids include rots or black tips to leaves, and these are cultural in their origin. Young growths are very susceptible to rotting in their centers, especially where water has remained for some time. Remove or cut away the rotted growth and dust the raw area with sulfur to dry it up. All wet rots can be treated in this way. Dry rots, such as black tips on the leaves, can be caused by a cultural fault such as cold, or a combination of cold and wet. It sometimes occurs where leaves have been touching or standing too close to the glass in the greenhouse. A plant which is in a generally poor condition will usually have black tips on its leaves. These can be trimmed back using a pruning knife, the blade of which has first been passed through a flame or dipped in methylated spirits in order to sterilize it. When the cultural problem has been improved the black areas will not spread any further into the green area. The occasional black tip on older foliage is nothing to be concerned about, but if all the leaves (including the youngest) are affected in this way, you will need to check that the temperature, humidity, and light levels are all in balance.

The same poor conditions will cause premature spotting on flowers, and will probably be the reason for pollen turning black, thus shortening the life of the flower. Large, oval, black or brown marks midway along the leaf's surface can often be traced to sunburn, particularly where there has been over-exposure in an unshaded area. Sun burn is caused by the sun's rays penetrating through the glass where there is insufficient shading. Suntan, where the foliage takes on a reddish hue, is also the result of too much sun, but here the foliage will return to a healthier green when the shading is increased. To a lesser extent, overall yellowing of the foliage can be caused through insufficient shading and is particularly noticeable on plants badly in need of repotting where there is no nourishment left in the compost. A regular foliar feed, as well as fresh compost, will rectify this.

Pseudobulbs are the water reserves for the plant, taken up by the roots. When water does not reach the pseudobulbs for some while, they will shrivel because the water is not being replaced. There can be two causes for this, overwatering or underwatering. Overwatering will cause the roots to die and therefore be unable to function by supplying the necessary water. Examine the roots and if they are found to be dead, remove them and repot the plant. If new roots are encouraged quickly, the plant will recover and the pseudobulbs will again be plump and healthy. Spray the foliage to prevent further moisture loss through the leaves. The underwatered plant requires less drastic and obvious action.

A further problem with pseudobulbs is where they can be seen to be getting smaller each year, which is the reverse of what it should be. There can be varied reasons for this, but most frequently it is because too many leafless pseudobulbs have been allowed to accumulate on the plant with detrimental results. By reducing the size of the plant and restoring the balance of more pseudobulbs in leaf than out of leaf, the plant should again make progress. A string of undersized pseudobulbs will also inhibit flowering, as their small size renders them unable to produce flower spikes. This condition can also be accompanied by premature leaf loss, which also adds to the problem. Against the odds, plants will sometimes bloom in this weakened condition. In this case, flowering should not be taken as a sign that all is well with the plant. Rather, it is a distress signal, the dying plant try-

Left: *Paphiopedilum* St. Swithin 'Winchester.' A fine hybrid which produces several flowers on a stem, with long thin petals that can measure over 6 inches (15 centimeters) from tip to tip.

ing one last time to perpetuate itself by using its remaining resources to produce seed.

Conditions under which orchids are less likely to thrive are extremes of temperature, either too hot or too cold. Orchids dislike being hot and dry, or cold and wet. Both extremes will cause stress, leading to other associated problems such as poor growth and lack of flowers.

Routine attention to your orchids will keep the plants looking good at all times.

One of the most exciting moments is when new flower spikes are first seen emerging from inside the basal leaf, or the apex of the pseudobulb. This is the climax to the cultural year and is confirmation that all has gone well.

Cymbidium flower spikes appear at the end of the growing season and develop throughout the winter months. When first seen, they appear identical to the new growths, but they are fatter, penciled, and continue to grow without fanning out into leaves. When they reach a height of 6–8 inches (about 20 centimeters) it will become necessary to support them by inserting a bamboo cane into the compost as close to the flower spike as possible. Keep the cane away from the rim of the pot where the roots are. Tie the flower spike to the cane to ensure it grows vertically and avoid the danger of it snapping under the eventual weight of a heavy crop of buds. Other orchids can be treated in the same way, with the smaller odontoglossums, miltoniopsis, and phalaenopsis needing lighter canes. These plants need their flower spikes supporting up to just below the buds. This will allow the flowers to arch naturally on the stem when they will look their best.

After flowering, the old spikes can be cut off near the base. You can also remove the old dried bracts encasing the pseudobulbs. To do this, split each one into two and peel down on either side of the pseudobulb, and then pull away. This will improve the appearance of the plant, and also ensure there are no unwanted pests such as earwigs lurking there. Broken leaves can be removed to enhance the plants appearance. Dead leaves which have been discarded by the plants should be collected and burnt. If left on the benches or allowed to rot under the staging, they will encourage further pests such as woodlice to breed there.

Opposite: *Masdevallia* Falcata 'Patrick.' These stunning orchids belong to the genus *Masdevallia,* with over 300 species.

PART TWO
AN A-Z
OF POPULAR
ORCHIDS

AERANGIS

Habitat
A genus of pretty and distinct species which originate throughout tropical Africa and Madagascar. Of the fifty or so epiphytic species only a few are in cultivation, generally in specialist collections. They are available as nursery raised seed and a few hybrids are sometimes found. The various species have different flowering times and most are fragrant.

Description
The plants are mostly small, producing narrow, rigid leaves from the center of a continually upward growing rhizome, and are evergreen. The flower spike comes from the base of a mature leaf with the flowers clear of the leaves. While some produce a single bloom, others have many flowered, drooping, or arching spikes which are often spectacular. The genus is characterized by the white, star shaped flowers with long spurs at the base of the lip which trail below the blooms, and which contain the nectar to attract the pollinating moth. Their size varies from 1–2 inches (2–5 centimeters) across, while the plants may be up to 6 inches (15 centimeters) tall.

Cultivation
Grow in a warm greenhouse with a good moist atmosphere and shade for most of the year. Water all year, apply feed in summer. Spray foliage in summer. Grow in half pots, shallow baskets, or on bark.

AERIDES

Habitat
A genus of pretty epiphytic, evergreen species which originate from Southeast Asia. Of the twenty or so known, only a few are in cultivation as they have become rare. They are usually available as nursery raised propagations. Those found in collections are mostly early summer flowering, and highly fragrant.

Description

The plants are of modest size. Long strap-like leaves are produced from the center of a continually upward growing rhizome. The flower spikes come from the base of the mature leaf. The spikes are arching, carrying many small, but extremely attractive flowers whose main colors are pink and white. Plants may be up to 12 inches (30 centimeters) tall, and the flowers 1–2 inches (2–5 centimeters) wide.

Cultivation
Grow in an intermediate greenhouse with good light all year round, but light shade in summer. Water and apply feed all year, less in winter. Spray foliage in summer to encourage aerial roots. The plants grow best in half pots, shallow baskets, or on bark.

Previous pages 52–53: *Odontocidium Tiger Butter.* **A hybrid made by crossing** *Odontoglossum* **and** *Oncidium,* **combining the best qualities from both parents.**

Far right: *Aerangis citrata.* **A pretty species which grows well in a warm greenhouse mounted on bark. It likes warm, moist conditions and produces its fragrant blooms in the late winter.**

ANGRAECUM

Habitat

A spectacular genus containing some very large species while others are very small. Most of the two hundred or so species are epiphytic, with some that are lithophytic or terrestrial. Their range is mainly throughout tropical Africa and Madagascar. A number of the select species are grown, available as nursery raised from seed. These bloom at different seasons of the year.

Description

The plants are mostly robust, producing pairs of long, straplike leaves from upward growing rhizomes. The flower spikes come from the base of the mature leaf and can carry a dozen or more stunning flowers of good size. These are characterized by their cool, white to pale green, glassy appearance and long spurs. The largest types can grow to 2 feet (60 centimeters) or more tall, with flower spikes of equal length and flowers 4 inches (10 centimeters) across, while the smallest are a mere 6 inches (15 centimeters) tall, with flowers less than a half inch (centimeter) across. Many are fragrant.

Above: *Angraecum eburnum* var. *superbum*. A warm-growing species which can grow to be quite tall. It needs plenty of room in shady conditions. It comes from Madagascar and blooms in winter.

Far left: *Aerides fieldingii*. A pretty species for the cool to intermediate greenhouse which grows well in a hanging basket. It is summer flowering and fragrant.

Cultivation

Grow in an intermediate to warm greenhouse, where they can be given shady conditions all year, with a high humidity in summer. Water and apply feed all year, less in winter. Spray foliage in summer. Grow the smaller species on bark, the larger ones in good sized pots.

Far left: *Anguloa clowesii*. This highly fragrant species is known as the 'Tulip Orchid' because of the shape of its flowers. It is cool growing and comes from Colombia.

ANGULOA

Habitat

A lovely genus of epiphytic and terrestrial species known as the Tulip Orchids because of the enclosed nature of the flowers. The ten or so species originate from parts of South America and are still grown to some extent in collections. They are spring to summer flowering and have a powerful fragrance.

Overleaf pages 60–61: *Barkeria skinnerii*. An autumn-flowering species from Central America that grows well in open slatted baskets; it will produce copious aerial roots in the summer.

Description

The plants produce robust green pseudobulbs with large, broad, supple leaves which are deciduous. The flowers appear singly on the stem which arises from the base of the latest pseudobulb before the new leaves are fully grown. Their colors are yellow, white, and pink. The plants when in full leaf will stand 3 feet (one meter) high while the flowers are 3–4 inches (7–10 centimeters) long. While the species are well worth growing, the variety is increased by a wide range of hybrids produced by the crossing with *Lycaste* which has produced the bigeneric hybrid *Angulocaste*, where the more open flowers are larger and the color range greater.

Cultivation

Grow in an intermediate greenhouse and allow plenty of headroom when in growth. Grow cooler in winter. Water well and apply feed in summer. Give little or no water while plants are dormant. Do not spray the foliage. Grow in pots and repot each year in spring. Give shade in summer and full light in winter.

Below: *Barkeria spectabilis*. A small-growing, delightful species for cool greenhouse or indoor growing. It likes a decided rest in the winter, when it becomes deciduous.

BARKERIA

Habitat

A small epiphytic genus comprising about ten neat species which originate from central America. A few of these are in general cultivation, available as nursery raised plants from seed. They bloom in the early summer.

Description

The plants produce slender, cane-like pseudobulbs with pairs of supple leaves along their length, which are deciduous. The pretty flowers are produced on slender stems which arise from the apex of the cane. The flowers are bright to pale pink with attractively marked lips, and the spikes are few to many flowered. In the spring the plants produce an explosion of aerial roots from the base which form an added attraction. The plants may reach 6–9 inches (14–23 centimeters) before flowering and the blooms can be less than one inch (2 centimeters) across.

Cultivation

Grow indoors or in a cool greenhouse. Water and apply feed during the summer, and allow plants to completely dry out in winter when leafless. Spray aerial roots in summer. Grow in open, slatted shallow baskets and repot each year in spring when new growth starts. Shade in summer and give full light in winter.

BRASSAVOLA

Habitat

A small genus of about 15 epiphytic, evergreen species which holds much interest for growers. The plants originate from the Americas and are popular for their cool green, slender petaled flowers and the sweet fragrance of some species. They are mainly summer flowering when the blooms last for several weeks.

Description

The plants produce thin, pencil-like stems with one or two rigid, terete leaves. The flower spikes emerge from the top of the stem at the base of the leaf. Several blooms are produced often assuming a pendent habit. The plants are not more than 6 inches (15 centimeters) tall, and the flowers can be 2 inches (5 centimeters) across. Aerial roots are also a feature of these plants which are at their best when grown on to specimen size when they will produce flowers for much of the year.

Cultivation

Grow indoors or in a cool to intermediate greenhouse in good light. Water sparingly at all times, even less in winter and apply feed in summer. spray whole plant in summer. Grow in shallow pans or preferably on bark or fiber slab.

BRASSIA

Habitat

A spectacular genus of about twenty-five epiphytic, evergreen species which originate from tropical America. A number of the species and a very few hybrids are extremely popular in cultivation. Nursery raised plants from seed can be obtained. They are mostly summer flowering, and the flowers are noted for their extraordinarily long – up to 6 inches (15 centimeters) – petals and sepals which give rise to their common name of Spider Orchids.

Description

The plants produce overall green pseudobulbs with two main leaves which are narrow of medium length. The flower spikes appear from inside the first leaf when the pseudobulb has matured. The plants are of medium size at about 12 inches (30 centimeters) tall. The flower spikes are taller, the dozen or so blooms held well clear of the foliage. Because of the length of the petals in some species, the flowers can reach 12 inches (30 centimeters) long. Some support may be necessary to prevent the flowers from touching the foliage.

Left: *Brassavola nodosa.* **A pretty species for the intermediate section. The plant blooms at various times and the fragrant flowers are long-lived. It comes from Central America.**

Brassia verrucosa. **A most attractive and free-flowering species for the cool greenhouse or indoors. It is very fragrant, flowering in early summer.**

Cultivation

Grow indoors or in a cool greenhouse in shady conditions with good air flow. Water and apply feed all year (less in winter), without allowing pseudobulbs to shriven. Spray in summer. Give full light in winter.

BULBOPHYLLUM

Habitat

This is a huge genus of upwards of one thousand epiphytic, evergreen species which are widely distributed in parts of the globe including Southeast Asia, Africa, and Australia, as well as tropical America. It is also one of the most diverse with strange, often bizarre species being commonplace. They are hugely interesting in a botanical way, but not often grown for their beauty. Numerous species are in cultivation which bloom at various times of the year.

Description

Most, but not all, are plants of small or modest size. They produce rounded pseudobulbs with a single, leathery leaf and the flowers are born on spikes which come from the base of the plant. The flowers may be solitary, or held in an umbel at the end of the stem, or along the length of the stem. Many strange features and adaptations can be seen in the flowers. Some are scented, often unpleasantly.

Cultivation

Selected species can be grown indoors, in a cool or intermediate greenhouse, in shady conditions with good light in winter. Water and apply feed in summer, less in winter. Spray in summer. Most are at their best when grown to specimen size and can be accommodated in wooden baskets suspended near the glass.

Bulbophyllum (Cirrhopetalum) **Elizabeth Ann 'Bucklebury.' There are over one thousand species of the genus** *Bulbophyllum* **in the Old World tropics.**

Calanthe vestita. **These lovely orchids shed their tall foliage in winter and bloom while they are resting. The flowers are very long lasting.**

CALANTHE

Habitat

A genus of about 150 mostly terrestrial species originating mainly from tropical Asia. They are divided into two groups, evergreen and deciduous. While the evergreen species are highly attractive and colorful, they are less well known than the deciduous types, which carry great favor in collections. The latter are known for their long, wistful flower spikes of white to pink flowers, which remain in bloom for long periods over the winter. Both hybrids and species are grown.

Description

The deciduous plants produce cone-shaped, silvery pseudobulbs which live for two years before dying, and large, flat supple leaves to 2 feet (60 centimeters) tall. The flower spikes which come from the base at the end of the growing season carry dozens of delightful flowers while the plant is leafless.

Cultivation

Keep cool in shady conditions throughout the summer. Give full light in winter. Water and apply feed liberally in summer, but dry out completely in winter. Separate the pseudobulbs while still in their pot after the leaves have been shed, when both will produce new growth. Do not spray foliage. Grow in pots and repot annually adding extra granulated feed to the base.

CATTLEYA

Habitat

The most beautifully flamboyant and popular genus including numerous intergeneric hybrids which are widely available. The epiphytic, evergreen species which originate from central America are mostly rare, and belong in specialized collections. The hybrids have enormous appeal and are well suited to the mixed collection.

Description

The plants produce tall, club-shaped or slender pseudobulbs with one or two semirigid leathery leaves and can be up to 3 feet (1 meter) tall, although miniature varieties are much smaller. The flowers, up to 4 inches (10 centimeters) across are produced from one to six on a stem arising from a protective sheath at the base of the leaf in spring or autumn. The

Cattleya loddigesii. This is a bi-foliate *Cattleya* species which produces its attractive blooms at any time of the summer. The plant originates from Central America.

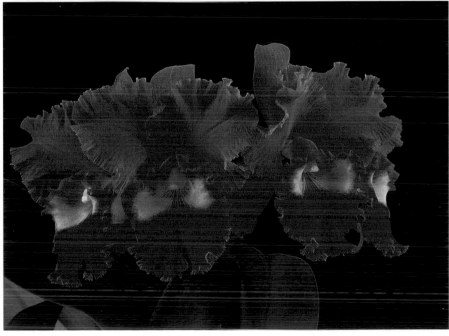

Above: *Brassolaeliocattleya* Rising Sun 'La Tuilerie.' The result of crossing *Brassavola*, *Laelia*, and *Cattleya*, with the qualites of all three.

Left: *Laeliocattleya* Drumbeat 'Triumph.' Few orchids equal the flamboyance of these wonderful hybrids which produce fragrant flowers during spring and autumn months.

Facing page top: *Potinara* Sunrise. A highly colored, scented plant, the result of crossing *Brassavola*, *Cattleya*, *Laelia*, and *Sophronitis*.

Facing page bottom: *Sophronitis coccinea*. Seen less and less in collections today, it has produced many fine hybrids.

Above: *Coelogyne cristata*. One of the very best of the *Coelogyne* species, this fine plant originates from India, and is easily grown and flowered indoors or in a cool greenhouse.

Previous pages 72–73: *Coelogyne fimbrata*. A compact growing species that can be grown in baskets or half pots. It is suitable for indoor growing, or a cool greenhouse. It flowers in the spring.

colors in the multitude of hybrids range through white, pink, and yellow to the most vibrant shades of lavender and cerise. The lips are large and frilly, and are often highlighted with other colorings.

Cultivation
Grow indoors or in an intermediate greenhouse in good light all year. Water and apply feed all year, but less in winter. Spray in summer.

COELOGYNE

Habitat
A delightful genus of over one hundred epiphytic, evergreen species originating from a wide area including Asia, India, and Indonesia. A number of

species and very few hybrids are grown. The plants vary enormously in size from very small plants which grow into huge mats, to tall impressive specimens over three feet (one meter) tall.

Description

The plants produce green pseudobulbs and a pair of narrow leaves, the flower spike coming from inside the new growth while very young. The flowers, which can be as small as a half-inch (one centimeter) or as large as 4 inches (10 centimeters) across are predominately white, often with a crystallized appearance, with cream, salmon, green, and yellow also represented. Various species bloom in the winter, spring, or early summer.

Cultivation

Coelogynes may be cool or intermediate growing, and are mostly suited to pot culture; although some of the smaller ones can be accommodated in suspended wooden slatted baskets where they can remain undisturbed for years, and allowed to grow into complete balls surrounding the basket. Grow in good light all year. Water and apply feed in summer, less in winter, allowing plants to dry out but not to shrivel. Spray in summer.

CYMBIDIUM

Habitat

A popular genus with a huge variety of hybrids. The forty-five mainly epiphytic species originate from India, Burma, and Thailand, as well as parts of Australia and elsewhere. Most are rare and have been replaced in contemporary collections by the multitude of hybrids which are available as meristemmed and seed raised plants. There are two main types, standard and miniature. While the standards give the larger flower, the miniatures are often more free flowering with a greater number of flowers on the spike.

Description

The plants produce rounded pseudobulbs with long, straplike evergreen leaves. The flower spike appears from the base of the youngest pseudobulb in late summer and will require supporting as it grows. The flowers, a dozen or more on the spike, open during the winter or spring and will last for eight to ten weeks. Their color range is from white, through pink, red, bronze, green, and yellow. The flowers can vary in size from 3–4 inches (8–10 centimeters) across. The plants can be 2–3 feet (60–90 centimeters) high with the flowers above the foliage.

Cultivation

Grow indoors or in a cool greenhouse. Place out of doors for the summer. Water and apply feed all year, less in winter. Spray foliage in summer. Shade in summer and give full light in winter. Too high temperatures can prevent flowering.

Cymbidium Lady Bug 'Drum.' A miniature type orchid that produces numerous flowers on upright spikes in the winter. Suitable for growing indoors or in a cool greenhouse.

Above: *Cymbidium* Kelpic. A miniature, free-flowering hybrid which produces its upright flower spikes during the winter. Suitable for growing indoors or in a cool greenhouse.

Left: *Cymbidium* Rincon 'Clarrisa'. A standard type hybrid which will bloom over a long period in the spring. Grow in a cool greenhouse and give planty of winter light to encourage flowers.

Far left: *Cymbidium* Nonina 'Paleface.' A miniature type hybrid which produces an abundance of flowers from upright spikes during winter and spring months. Suitable for a cool greenhouse or grown indoors.

DACTYLORHIZA

Habitat

An attractive terrestrial genus which includes about forty species distributed throughout Europe and the Mediterranean as well as other temperate parts of the world. These hardy plants can be cultivated in gardens and under glass, but are not without their problems. They are notorious for building up large colonies one year and producing very few plants the next. They are included here to represent a typical ground orchid which grows almost anywhere in temperate climates and is exciting to find growing naturally often in huge numbers over a wide area, where they must not be disturbed. Take only photographs!

Description

The plants produce leafy, upright stems which terminate in a flowering spike in early summer. The whole plant dies down for the winter after producing seed. Underground tubers are produced which sustain the plant from one season to the next.

Cultivation

If you think you could grow ground orchids, nursery raised plants are available from specialist nurseries.

Far left: *Dactylorhiza elata.* A spectacular terrestrial species that grows in Europe and parts of Africa. It can be cultivated where conditions outside are suitable.

Below: *Dactylorhiza foliosa.* This hardy terrestrial species comes from Mederia and can be cultivated where outside conditions permit. In flower the plant stands over 2 feet (60 centimeters) tall.

Above: *Dendrobium nobile.* A tall-growing attractive species from India, which blooms in the spring following a winter's rest.

Far right: *Dendrobium densiflorum.* This showy species from India produces its golden yellow flowers in drooping trusses during the spring. The plants produce tall, elongated pseudobulbs known as canes, and flower from the top.

DENDROBIUM

Habitat

A deservedly well-loved genus of greatly varying, mainly deciduous, mostly epiphytic species. Approximately nine hundred occur in many parts of the world, the most widely grown originating from India, Southeast Asia, Australia, and New Guinea. All are spectacular, some grotesquely so, but mostly they are extremely showy. Some species are grown but more often modern hybrids have taken their place. In particular, hybrids raised from *Dendrobium nobile* have produced some of the most colorful of all cultivated orchids, and can be found in a wide range of delightful color combinations featuring white, yellow, pink, and red. In cultivation these plants have become evergreen.

Description

The above hybrids produce tall, jointed pseudobulbs leafed along their length. The flowers are grouped on short stems along the pseudobulbs in the spring and early summer. The flowers have wide, overlapping sepals and petals with generous lips of a different hue. The plants can reach a height of 18 inches (45 centimeters) and the flowers are 2–3 inches (5–7 centimeters) across.

Above: *Encyclia fausta.* **A free-flowering, easy-to-grow, cool climate species which produces highly scented flowers in the early summer. Suitable for indoors, in a well-lit area.**

Cultivation

Grow in a cool greenhouse in good light. Place outdoors for the summer. Water and apply feed in summer, but only water in winter if pseudobulbs shrivel. Commence watering only after buds have formed, otherwise, if watered too early, growths will appear instead of flowers.

ENCYCLIA

Habitat

A genus of about 150, mainly epiphytic, evergreen species which originate from Mexico and elsewhere. A good number of the species are grown from nursery raised plants, while a few hybrids are occasionally seen. The species are delightful, and vary considerably. They can be loosely divided into two types. The first type are of modest size with elongated pseudobulbs which produce creamy-white to green flowers densely packed on an upright spike. The second type produce harder, rounded to cone-shaped pseudobulbs with tall spikes, loosely flowered. Both produce their flowers from the top of the pseudobulb. The former are exceedingly pretty and often fragrant. The latter have more somber shades of yellow, buff, and red-brown.

Description

The plants can be very small, a mere 2 inches (5 centimeters) tall, with solitary flowers of a half inch (one centimeter), or 12 inches (30 centimeters) high, with a flower spike adding another 18 inches (45 centimeters)

Encyclia nemorale. **A robust species from Central America which can be grown in a cool or intermediate greenhouse. The flowers appear in early summer.**

with all sizes in between. The smaller species are best grown on into large mats covering a small pan, while the larger species need pots. They bloom at different times, but mostly in the summer months.

Cultivation
Most grow cool, smaller types indoors or in a greenhouse. Water and apply feed in summer, give less in winter. Give shade in summer, full light in winter. The larger, hardbulbed species can be grown outdoors in the summer.

Far left: *Encyclia vitellina*. This richly-colored species from Mexico can be grown in a cool greenhouse, where it will bloom in the autumn.

EPIDENDRUM

Habitat
This is a large and varied genus containing some several hundred evergreen, epiphytic, and terrestrial species with a few hybrids having been raised. The plants produce tall, reed-type canes, leafed along their length which in some species can attain a height of several feet or meters. They flower from extended stems which may produce one, or more often, many flowers. Predominant colors are green, red, pink, and shades in-between. Some are brightly colored while others are more somber.

Description
The smallest are no more than 2 inches (5 centimeters) tall, and can be grown into large mats to cover a piece of bark or treefern fiber. The tallest are more suitable for an area with plenty of headroom, when the flowering spikes on some will remain in bloom for months on end. The flowering time varies with the species.

Below: *Epidendrum stamfordianum*. A cool to intermediate species which likes to be grown in good light. It flowers in summer and originated in South America.

Laelia anceps. **A pretty, autumn flowering species for the cool greenhouse or indoor culture. The plant flowers during the autumn, producing blooms from a tall flower spike.**

Cultivation

Most are cool growing, but the larger varieties need space to grow and can become considerably large. Water and apply feed in summer, give less in winter. Grow in good light all year.

LAELIA

Habitat

A lovely genus of evergreen, epiphytic species closely related to the cattleyas. About fifty species originate from parts of South and central America. Some of the species are becoming rare in collections, but there are numerous intergeneric hybrids which have greatly extended the range of colors, which include white, pink, yellow, orange, and red.

Description
Although varied, they typically produce elongated pseudobulbs with a single thick, leathery leaf. The flower spike emerges from the apex of the pseudobulb and carries from one to several flowers. There is much variation in the size of plants and flowers, giving rise to distinct miniature and standard types among the hybrids. Their flowering times vary with the seasons, depending upon their origins. They can be either cool or intermediate growing.

Cultivation
Both types are suitable for indoors or a greenhouse. Water and apply feed in summer, less in winter. Do not allow pseudobulbs to shrivel. Spray in summer. Larger varieties may be placed outdoors in the summer.

LYCASTE

Habitat
These can be epiphytic, lithophytic, or terrestrial. There are about twenty-five species spread mainly throughout South America. A number of the species are popular in collections, as well as numerous hybrids which include bigeneric hybrids crossed with *Anguloa*. All are deciduous.

Description
The main color range is through white, yellow, green, and brown. The plants produce green, cone-shaped pseudobulbs with several large, ribbed,

Above: *Lycaste aquila 'Detente.'* A cool-growing hybrid which can produce numerous flowers on single spikes during the spring. It sheds most of its foliage during the winter.

Left: *Lycaste* Wyld Court. An exceptionally dark-flowered hybrid which produces single flowers in the spring. The plant is cool growing and rests in the winter.

Overleaf: *Masdevallia rosea* 'Nadine.' An attractive species from South America which flowers prolifically during the summer. The single-flowered stems are taller than the leaves.

and supple leaves. The flowering stems which appear from the base of the pseudobulb can be numerous, each carrying a solitary, boldly colored bloom. Their main flowering time is spring and early summer. The plants can be 12 inches (30 centimeters) tall when in leaf with 3 inch (8 centimeter) triangular flowers below the foliage.

Cultivation
Grow indoors or in a cool greenhouse in shady conditions with full light in winter. Water and apply feed in summer. Allow to dry out in winter, but do not allow to shrivel. Do not spray the foliage.

MASDEVALLIA

Habitat
A large genus of about 340 delightful, modest sized evergreen epiphytic or sometimes lithophytic species, which originate from South America. A number of the species are in cultivation together with a good choice of colorful hybrids. The typically triangular flowers, often with long tails to the sepals, give rise to the common name of Kite Orchids.

Description
The neat plants produce short stems with a single, semirigid leaf. The flower spike may carry one, or several eye-catching flowers whose colors range from yellow, pink, gold, and bronze shades through rich cerise. Their size varies from small plants 2 inches (5 centimeters) high to others over 12 inches (30 centimeters) when in flower. They bloom mainly during the summer months.

Cultivation
Grow indoors or in a cool greenhouse in shady conditions all year. Water all year, and apply feed in summer. Do not spray foliage. Grow in small pots, but avoid drying out completely.

MAXILLARIA

Habitat
A genus of about three hundred evergreen, epiphytic, or lithophytic species, a number of which are very popular in collections. They originate from parts of central and South America. Very few hybrids have been produced to equal the prettier species.

Description
The plants are extremely various, but most are neat, producing small pseudobulbs with one or more leaves. The flowers are typically triangular, with narrow or broad petals and sepals. Many are strongly scented. The color range is from white through yellows and red-browns, often with dense spotting. The smallest plants can be 6 inches (15 centimeters) high and the largest over 12 inches (30 centimeters) with the flowers appearing singly on short stems.

Left: *Maxillaria rufescens*. A miniature species suitable for the cool greenhouse or indoor culture. The plant originates from South America and is best grown into a large plant.

Cultivation

Grow smaller varieties indoors, or in a cool greenhouse. Water and apply feed all year, less in winter. Grow in shade during the summer and give full light in winter. Spray foliage in summer. These are at their best when grown into specimen size. Some can be grown in baskets or on bark.

MILTONIOPSIS

Habitat

A very beautiful genus of only five, mainly epiphytic, evergreen species which originate from central and South America. While the species are rare and have become collector's items, there is a multitude of charming hybrids which have greatly extended the colors available from white, yellow, and pink, to the most vibrant dark reds, all with variously colored masks on their lips. These are available as meristemmed plants, or seed raised. The large, flat flowers are affectionately called Pansy Orchids. They all have fragrance.

Description

The plants produce green, oval pseudobulbs each with several long, narrow supple leaves, 9–12 inches (20–30 centimeters) long. The flower spikes come from inside the basal leaf and carry up to six large, 4 inch (10 centimeters) wide, showy flowers. They have two main flowering seasons, blooming twice a year in early summer and autumn when the flowers will last for several weeks. The flower spikes will require some support while growing.

Cultivation

Grow indoors or in a cool greenhouse. Water and apply feed all year, less in winter. Do not spray the foliage. Keep shaded all year, less in winter.

Below: *Miltoniopsis* Emotion. A distinctly colored variety which can be grown indoors or in a cool greenhouse. The plants can be very free-flowering.

Left: *Miltoniopsis* Petunia 'Red Admiral.' This richly colored hybrid is an ideal beginner's orchid. It grows well indoors and will bloom twice a year.

Far left: *Maxillaria tenuifolia*. An elegant species from Central America which grows well in a cool greenhouse or indoors. It does best when grown on bark.

Right: *Miltoniopsis* Rouge 'California Plum.' This fine, modern hybrid will bloom in the autumn and early summer. Its compact size and large flowers make it ideal for indoor culture.

Above: *Miltoniopsis* Robert Strauss 'Snow White.' These large, flamboyant, and fragrant flowers are produced on a modest sized plant, making it ideal for indoors.

ODONTOGLOSSUM

Habitat

A highly decorative and popular large genus containing about sixty ever-green, epiphytic species, most of which are collector's plants. More suited to the mixed collection are the multitude of excellent hybrids which have been produced, often including closely related genera to give multigeneric hybrids which have greatly extended the color range to include all except blue. Varieties with exquisite markings and patterns shine alongside the self-colored types. Meristemms are available as well as seed raised plants.

Description

The plants produce green pseudobulbs with long, narrow leaves up to 12 inches (30 centimeters). The flower spikes, often carrying a dozen or more flowers come from inside the first basal leaf and can be 18 inches (45 centimeters) tall. They will require some support as they grow. Their flowering

Above: *Odontioda* Dalmar 'Lyoth Baachus.' A richly colored hybrid produced by crossing *Odontoglossum* and *Cochlioda*. The latter genus has contributed to the red coloring.

Right: *Rossioglossum (Odontoglossum) grande*. A sought-after species from Guatemala which is becoming rare in collections. The richly-colored flowers will appear in the autumn.

season is year round, with a peak in the spring. Although there is wide variation in the flowers, the numerous inter-related plants are similar in appearance. All are loosely grouped under the name odontoglossums.

Cultivation

Grow indoors or in a cool greenhouse. Water and apply feed all year, less in winter. Do not allow pseudobulbs to shrivel. Spray lightly in summer. Keep shaded all year, less in winter, and ventilate well.

ONCIDIUM

Habitat

A genus of epiphytic, lithophytic, or terrestrial, evergreen plants with as many as about four hundred species spread over tropical America. The most attractive species are in general cultivation together with a good

Below: *Lemboglossum (Odontoglossum) bictoniense.* This elegant species from Mexico produces tall flower spikes in the early spring. It is an easy-to-grow plant for indoors or a cool greenhouse.

Overleaf page 98: *Odontioda* Jumbo 'Mont Millais.' A fine modern hybrid from the Odontoglossum group. The plant is cool growing and can bloom at almost any time.

Overleaf page 99: *Vuylstekeara* Cambria 'Plush.' A richly-colored and popular hybrid produced from crossing *Cochlioda, Miltonia (Miltoniopsis),* and *Odontoglossum.* An ideal beginner's orchid.

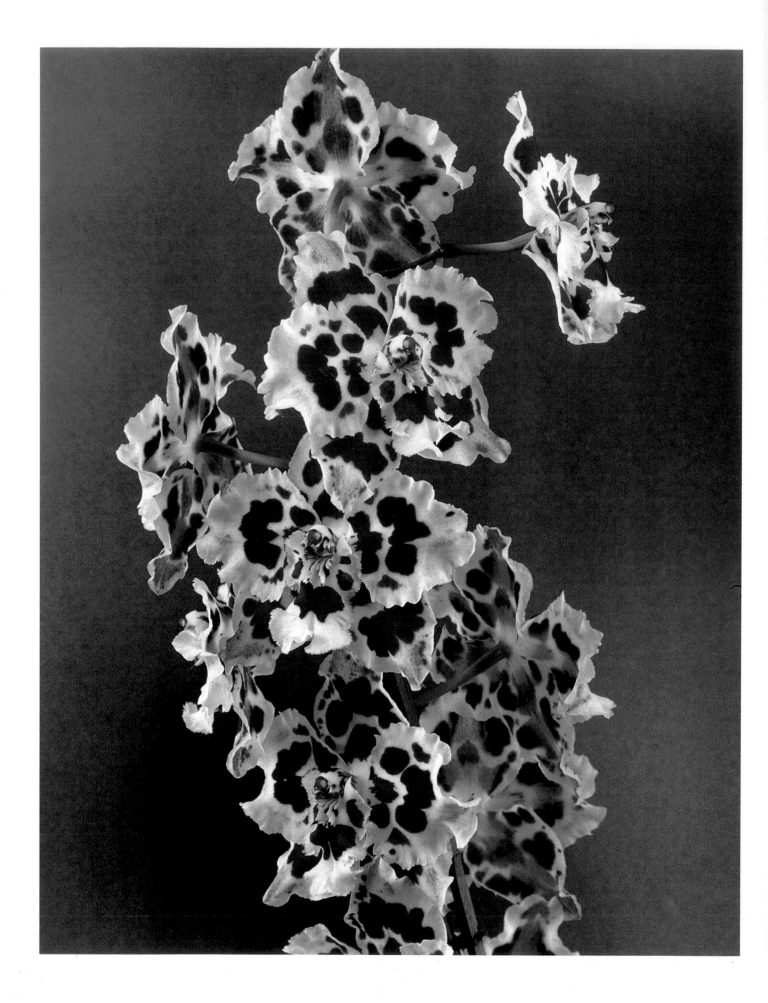

number of hybrids, many intergeneric. These are available as nursery raised from seed, or meristemmed plants.

Description

The plants vary considerably in habit, but typically the more popular varieties have green, oval pseudobulbs with long, narrow, and supple leaves. The smaller types are less then 6 inches (15 centimeters) high, while others can be considerably taller. The flower spikes come from inside the basal leaf and may be up to 6 feet (2 meters) but are more typically 2 feet (60 centimeters). The dainty blooms can be 2–3 inches (5–8 centimeters) across, with the enlarged, flat lip being the most predominant part of the flower. Their color range is mainly yellow, with pink and brown shades also seen. Their flowering season can vary, and many bloom during the autumn.

Cultivation

Grow indoors or, depending upon the type, in a cool or intermediate greenhouse in good light all year. Water and apply feed in summer, less in winter. Some varieties have an upward growing habit and are best suited to bark culture.

Far left: *Odontoglossum crispum*. A beautiful species from South America which has been bred over many years to improve and enlarge the pure white flowers.

Below: *Oncidium flexuosum*. This attractive species carries its small, bright yellow flowers in a cluster at the top of a tall spike in autumn. It will grow indoors, or in a cool to intermediate greenhouse.

PAPHIOPEDILUM

Habitat

This is a distinct genus containing about sixty-five evergreen, mainly terrestrial species which originate from Southeast Asia, China, the Philippines, and elsewhere. The modification of the lip into a pouch has earned these plants the common name of Slipper Orchids. While a number of the species are in cultivation, more suited to the amateur's collection is a selection from the multitude of hybrids which are available as seed grown plants.

Description

The plants produce growths, each consisting of several leaves, which are typically thick and leathery, long and narrow, lacking pseudobulbs. The flowering stem arises from the center of the mature growth and may carry one to many flowers up to 4 inches (10 centimeters) across. These may have short or long petals, in the latter greatly enlarging the actual flower size. Their color range has been extended to include white, yellow, pink, green, red, and some of the deepest purple shades in the orchid family. Typically plants may be 12 inches (30 centimeters) wide, the flowering stem standing above the foliage. The foliage may be self-colored green, or mottled in light and dark green. They also produce some of the most dramatic flowers. The flowering season is various, and the blooms last for several months.

Far left: *Psychopsis (Oncidium) papilio.* One of the strangest orchid flowers, known as the 'Butterfly Orchid.' The plant blooms over a long period in the summer, flowering in succession.

Below: *Paphiopedilum venustum.* This elegant species from India blooms in the autumn and winter, and can be grown either indoors or in a cool greenhouse.

Cultivation

Grow in a warm room or intermediate greenhouse in good shade all year. Water and apply feed all year, less in winter. Do not spray foliage.

Above: *Paphiopedilum* Obi Major. An attractive hybrid, this vigorous grower will bloom during the early winter, and the blooms will last for many weeks.

PHALAENOPSIS

Habitat

This is a lovely genus of about forty-six evergreen, epiphytic, or lithophytic species which originate from the Philippines, Southeast Asia, and elsewhere. The species are not so common in collections, having been superseded by thousands of beautiful hybrids which are available as seed raised plants, or stem propagations. There are two main types, the standard and

Far left: *Paphiopedilum* Danella 'Chilton.' This very fine hybrid shows the well-rounded flower carried on a tall stem well above the foliage.

miniature. The standards can reach a height of 3 feet (one meter) when in bloom, while the miniatures are less than 12 inches (30 centimeters) in bloom. Both types produce similar plants which have broad, flashy leaves arising from the center of the continually growing plant. The shedding of the lower, older leaves allows the plants to remain small, with four to five leaves at any time.

Description

The standard flowers, 3 inches (8 centimeters) across are produced on long, often branching and arching spikes of a dozen or more white or pink flowers. The miniature types are smaller, on shorter branching spikes, and their color range is white, pink, and yellow, often striped or spotted in attractive hues. Their flowering season is various, and it is not unusual for one plant to bloom three times in one year. By reducing the length of the stem after flowering, it is possible to have a secondary flowering from a lower node, thus extending the flowering season even further. Tallest spikes will need supporting.

Cultivation

Grow in a warm room or greenhouse in shade. Water and apply feed all year, less in winter. Do not spray foliage.

Far left: *Paphiopedilum* St. Swithin 'Winchester.' One of the multi-flowered hybrids which produce flowers with extended petals. The plants are robust and need a shady position in an intermediate greenhouse.

Below: *Paphiopedilum* Honda Hall. These yellow-flowered hybrids are very popular plants for the intermediate greenhouse. Their long-lasting flowers appear mainly during the winter months.

Above: *Phalaenopsis amboinensis.* A warm growing species from Sumatra that produces flowers from short spikes, in succession over a long period.

Far right: *Phragmipedium* Grande Macrochilum Giganteum. An extraordinary species with ribbon-like petals that can reach over 12 inches (30 centimeters).

PHRAGMIPEDIUM

Habitat
This is an outstanding genus of over a dozen, mainly terrestrial, evergreen and often spectacular species which originate mainly from South America. Related to the paphiopedilums they are included among the Slipper Orchids. While the species are not often seen in cultivation, modern hybrids are becoming available in a beautiful range of red shades. These

plants can attain a height of 4 feet (one and a half meters) when in bloom, and need plenty of headroom in their growing area.

Description

The plants produce robust growths each consisting of several long, strap-like leaves. The flowering stems come from the center of the mature growth and may carry several blooms, often flowering in succession over a long period. The flowers can be typically 5 inches (12 centimeters) across, and in some varieties very much longer where they produce long, ribbon-like extended petals. Reds and browns predominate this genus. Their flowering season is extensive, and many bloom in the spring.

Cultivation

Grow in a warm greenhouse in shade all year. Water and apply feed all year, less in winter. Do not spray foliage.

PLEIONE

Habitat

An extremely attractive genus of terrestrial or lithophytic deciduous species which originate mainly from India, China, and Formosa. Less than twenty species are found, most of which are in cultivation, available as nursery propagated plants. Numerous hybrids have extended the color range in shades of white, yellow, and pink, to cerise.

Description

The plants produce cone or bottle-shaped green pseudobulbs with a single long, wide leaf, which is shed at the end of the growing season. The flowers appear singly from the inside of the new growth while it is very young, in the spring. These are 1–2 inches (2–5 centimeters) across, and last about ten days. Plants in leaf and in bloom are about 6 inches (15 centimeters) tall. The pseudobulbs are short-lived, dying naturally after two years. A group of pseudobulbs should be grown together in a pan for the best effect.

Cultivation

Grow indoors or in a cold greenhouse with a minimum winter temperature five degrees above freezing. Keep cool in summer. Water and apply feed in summer, allow to remain dry in winter. Do not spray foliage. Grow in good light. Repot annually after flowering but before the new roots start. Do not bury the pseudobulbs.

POLYSTACHYA

Habitat

A genus of about 150 mainly modest-sized, evergreen, epiphytic, or lithophytic species which originate from Africa. The charming little flowers ensure they remain in cultivation, while few hybrids are generally seen. The color range extends from white, through yellow, green, and pink.

Description

The plants produce variously sized elongated, slender pseudobulbs with from one to several long, narrow leaves. The flower spike comes from the apex of the pseudobulb and carries numerous flowers on branching stems, notable for their upturned lips. The plants may be 6 inches (15 centimeters) tall, or more when in bloom, the flowers usually a half inch (one centimeter) across. Their flowering season is various, mostly throughout the summer.

Cultivation

Grow indoors or in a cool greenhouse. Water and apply feed all year, less in winter. Give shade in summer and good light in winter. Spray foliage lightly in summer.

Above: *Pleione formosana* 'Snow White.' A semi-hardy terrestrial species that grows best in a frost-free 'alpine' greenhouse. The flowers appear in spring.

Overleaf pages 110–111: *Pleione* Versailles. This hybrid can be grown indoors on a cool windowsill. The flowers arrive in spring after the plant's dormant period.

RHYNCHOSTYLIS

Habitat

A delightful evergreen, epiphytic genus of twelve species mainly from India and elsewhere. A few of the species are in cultivation with some hybrids having been produced. A number of these are intergeneric and have given rise to a much wider range of colors and flower styles.

Description

The plants produce an upward growing rhizome from which new leaves appear at the apex and aerial roots extend from the lower portion. The leaves are horizontal, stiffened to between 6–12 inches (15–30 centimeters) long, depending upon the variety. The flowers appear on densely packed, drooping spikes from the base of the mature leaf. They can be one inch (2.5 centimeters) or more across, and the main colors are white and pink shades through to red and blue.

Far left: *Polystachya odorata.* An attractive species from Africa which can be grown indoors or in a cool greenhouse. The plant is very free-flowering during the summer months.

Below: *Rhynchostylis gigantea* 'Petotiana.' A warm-growing species that likes good light all year round. Will grow well in an open basket hung close to the greenhouse glass.

Cultivation

Grow in an intermediate to warm greenhouse in good shade, with more light in winter. Maintain a high humidity. Water and apply feed all year, less in winter. These plants will make copious aerial roots which are thick and fleshy and are therefore best grown in wooden slatted baskets suspended in the greenhouse roof.

STANHOPEA

Habitat

An amazing genus of about 25 large, evergreen, mainly epiphytic species originating from central and South America. Their flowers are among the most unusual of orchids, but they are not unattractive, and are highly scented. Quite a few of the species are in cultivation, grown from seed. A few hybrids are also available. Their colors include white, cream, yellow, and red. The flowers are often splashed and dotted with additional colorings. It is the curious shape of the blooms which commands the most attention.

Description

The robust plants produce cone-shaped ribbed pseudobulbs with a solitary broad, flat, and stiffened leaf, to 12 inches (30 centimeters) long. The flower

Stanhopea tigrina. **This unusual species from South America grows in an open slatted basket and flowers beneath the plant. The downward spikes carry their large, but short-lived, flowers in the summer. It is highly scented.**

spikes come from the base and grow downward, often directly through the compost to flower beneath the plant. Up to six extraordinary flowers, 4 inches (10 centimeters) across are produced which will last three to four days. A succession of flower spikes opening at different times on a large plant will ensure an extended flowering period. They bloom mainly in the summer.

Vanda **Patricia Low 'Lydia.' An attractive hybrid for the warm greenhouse where it needs plenty of light and high humidity.**

Cultivation

Grow in a cool greenhouse in good light all year. Water and apply feed while plants are growing, usually in winter. Give less water in summer if resting. Spray foliage in summer. Grow in wooden slatted baskets to give free access to the developing flower spikes.

Vanda tricolor var. *'suavis.'* A tall-growing, free-flowering species for the intermediate to hot greenhouse.

VANDA

Habitat
A lovely genus of epiphytic or lithophytic evergreen species originating from India, Southeast Asia as well as New Guinea, Australia, and elsewhere. There are over thirty species, some of which are in general cultivation. Many more hybrids are available, some of these intergeneric crosses. The hybrids have greatly increased the variety and color of the flowers, which include exotic combinations of red and brown, blue and indigo, yellow and orange, and others. Blue is the most popular color of this group.

Description
The plants produce stiffened leaves from the apex of an upward growing rhizome, and plants can grow to 2–3 feet (60–90 centimeters) tall. The flower spikes come from the base of the mature leaves and carry up to half a dozen large, flat blooms which may be 4 inches (10 centimeters) across. Typically the sepals and petals are well rounded with a small, neat lip. The flowers are produced mainly in the spring and autumn.

Cultivation
Grow in a warm greenhouse in good light. Water and apply feed all year, less in winter. Spray the whole plant in summer. These grow best in wooden slatted baskets suspended near the glass, when copious aerial roots will be made. Maintain a high humidity.

ZYGOPETALUM

Habitat
A handsome genus of about forty evergreen, epiphytic species which originate from South America. A few of the species are grown alongside a good number of exciting hybrids. Their main coloration is a combination of green, brown, and purple. Some are available as meristemmes or seed raised plants.

Description
The plants are of medium size, producing oval pseudobulbs with two main, long and narrow leaves to 18 inches (45 centimeters), although others may be smaller. The flower spikes come from the base of the leading pseudobulb in late summer and carry up to a dozen dramatic flowers which may be very well scented. These are usually about 2 inches (5 centimeters) across, and appear mainly in the autumn.

Cultivation
Grow in a cool to intermediate greenhouse in shade, with more light in winter. Water and apply feed all year, but less in winter.

Do not spray foliage. The plants can be grown outdoors for the summer months.

Far left: *Vanda* Rothschildiana. One of the few orchids which are blue coloured. This hybrid grows and flowers well in the warm greenhouse in good light with a high humidity.

Following pages:
Page 122: *Ascocenda* Yip Sum Wah 'Tilgates Orange.' This hybrid is produced by crossing *Ascocentrum* – which gives it its rich color – with *Vanda*.

Page 123: *Zygopetalum* Blackii. This is a cool growing hybrid which grows quite tall. The flowers are produced in the autumn, and are nicely fragrant. It is cool growing.

Right: *Laelia gouldiana.* A cool-growing species from Mexico suitable for indoors or a cool greenhouse. The flowers will appear in the autumn and are carried on a tall spike.

URTHER READING

A Golden Guide to Orchids, 1989, American Orchid Society.

Home Orchid Growing, Northen, 1986, New York.

The Manual of Cultivated Orchid Species, Bechel, Cribb, Launert, 1992, Blandford/Cassell.

Orchids for Everyone, Williams et. al., 1980, Salamander.

You can Grow Orchids, Mary Noble, 1987, Florida.

JOURNALS:

Orchids - Journal of the American Orchid Society
6000 South Olive St., West Palm Beach, FL33405-4199, USA.

The Orchid Review - Journal of the Royal Horticultural Society
PO Box 38, Ashford, Kent, TN25 6PR, England.

OTHER TITLES BY THE AUTHOR:

Exotic Orchids, 1988, Salamander.

Growing your own Orchids, 1987, Salamader.

Orchid growing illustrated, 1994, Blandford Press.

Orchids as House Plants, 1989, Ward Lock/Cassell.

Orchids in Colour, 1994, Blandford Press.

Step-by-step guide to Growing and Displaying Orchids,
1993, Whitecap Books.

INDEX